The Great Famine
A Church of Ireland Perspective

APCK

DUBLIN 1996

First published in 1996 by
APCK
St Anne's, Dawson Street, Dublin 2

Cover by Bill Bolger
Origination by The Columba Press
Printed in Ireland by Paceprint Ltd, Dublin

ISBN: 1 899045 00 7

*The cover design is based on a detail
of the chancel arch, St Mary's Cathedral, Tuam.*

Table of Contents

Foreword   *Kenneth Milne*   4

1.   A Bitter Legacy?
        Patrick Comerford   5
2.   The Role of the Clergy in the Great Famine
        Robert McCarthy   9
3.   Church of Ireland mortality during the famine
        Cormac Ó Gráda   13
4.   Famine in today's world
        Bet Aalen   17
5.   Looking at the past
        Kenneth Milne   23

The Great Famine   *Most Reverend Dr Robin Eames*   26

Appendix: Ecumenical Service of Remembrance   28

The Contributors   39

Foreword

It is entirely appropriate that the Church of Ireland should participate in the commemoration of the Great Famine of 1845-7. This is so partly as a recognition of the dreadful suffering, physical and mental, endured by so many Irish people at that time; partly as a contribution to better understanding of the causes, course and consequences of that dire event which has been deemed a watershed in Irish history. How apt it would be if the commemoration likewise were to mark a watershed in our perception of the catastrophe itself, finding expression in due acknowledgement of sins of omission and commission where this has been lacking, and, equally in acknowledgement of humanitarian concern and activity where these have been overlooked .

So it was that the editor of *The Church of Ireland Gazette*, in an attempt to sharpen the focus of our perception, commissioned a series of articles on the Great Famine, which he is kindly allowing us to reproduce here. But, as a church, it was important that our response – and that of other Irish people – to the famine should find a liturgical mode of expression. This was provided by the diocese of Tuam, Killala and Achonry, when leaders of state and church met in St Mary's Cathedral in Tuam on Sunday 3 September 1995 for an act of worship that was broadcast by RTÉ Radio. The sermon preached by the Archbishop of Armagh forms part of this collection of papers: the order of service comprises the appendix.

APCK records with much appreciation subventions towards the cost of this publication received from the Minister of State at the Department of the Taoiseach and Chairperson of the Famine Commemoration Committee, Ms. Avril Doyle, and from the Standing Committee of the General Synod, through the APB Royalties Fund.

Kenneth Milne
Historiographer of the Church of Ireland

A Bitter Legacy?

Patrick Comerford

The Great Famine of 1845 to 1849 left a bitter legacy in many parts of Ireland. Memories still linger generations later of enforced migration and emigration, the loss of whole families and communities and the bitter regret of hopes that remained unfulfilled.

In many provincial and rural areas, the famine also left bitter memories of evangelical missionaries and their fervour. Whether the vigour and vitriol were real or imaginary is irrelevant in many communities, even today; what is real is the bitter, lingering memory.

It is an era that has left us with a language of myth and of prejudice: words like 'souper' and 'jumper', nicknames that still follow families for generations.

Today, thankfully, we live in more enlightened and ecumenical times. Today, hopefully, we can approach history without the burden of myth and popular misconceptions and we can appreciate the missionaries and their fervour in the context of their times. But, in many places it is still futile to argue like this: the popular myth and misconception still stand in the way of a realistic evaluation of the contribution of the missionaries of the time.

The famine coincided with a time that also saw some of the greatest controversies surrounding the evangelical missions in places like Achill Island, Co Mayo and Ventry in Co Kerry and the work of Alexander Dallas in Connemara.

In 1846, the potato blight reached Achill and in the following years the method of dispensing famine relief became a major source of ill-will. In 1848 and 1849, there was a huge increase in the number of converts reported in Achill and Edward Nangle never denied or apologised for the manner in which his missionary colony dispensed famine relief. Nevertheless, Nangle ordered a shipload of meal worth £3,000 for the island in its first famine winter and with the rector of Achill, Charles Seymour, he travelled to England to raise funds that enabled his missionary colony to employ 2,192 labourers and to feed 600 children a day.

Those who would detract from the Achill Mission are in danger of failing to point out that both Nangle and the supportive Bishop of Tuam, Thomas Plunket, had in many respects, a perfect foil in John MacHale, the Roman Catholic Archbishop of Tuam.

As Irene Whelan has pointed out, at the beginning of the last century 'Mayo was not especially renowned for its Catholic character and Achill was one of the most neglected areas of the west with reference to clerical manpower.'

This clerical neglect was coupled with neglect in the fields of education and health care. Dr Neason Adams left a profitable medical practice in Dublin in 1834 to spend a life caring for the poor people of Achill until his death in 1859. Nangle's first objective was to establish a school system, starting with an infant school at Slievemore, followed by schools in Dugort, Cashel and Keel. Without the educational efforts of Nangle's missionaries in Dugort, it is unlikely MacHale would have sent the Vincentian missionaries, Villas and Rinolfi, to the island with the hopes of launching a 'Second Counter-Reformation' or the Franciscans to Bunacurry to start a monastery and open a school, giving Achill two, albeit competing, educational systems.

On the other hand, Nangle's defenders have often been evangelicals of the most fervent type who have failed to appreciate that his approach to missionary work was often ahead of its time, with work that would later be identified with those who advocated a 'Social Gospel' or even 'Liberation Theology'.

The Achill missionaries were the first to build schools, a hospital and a dispensary on an island that had long gone without health care and educational facilities, so that Dr Adams became known as the 'St Luke of Achill'. They introduced crop rotation and land reclamation in an area over-burdened with rural poverty; and although the Irish language was in decline on the east coast, they taught through Irish, and in an area of high illiteracy introduced a printing press capable of publishing in Irish, as well as English, Hebrew, Greek and Latin.

Historians concerned with the activities of missionaries in West Kerry and Connacht have often paid little attention to another aspect of missionary interests in the Church of Ireland at the same time: the area of overseas mission.

In many of the years before the famine, the Hibernian Church Missionary Society often sent few missionaries overseas: in 1825, 1826, 1827, 1829, 1833, 1839, 1840, 1843, 1844 and 1845, only one man from Ireland went overseas each year on behalf of the CMS; in each of the years 1828, 1830, 1831, 1834, 1836, 1838, 1841 and 1842, no men went abroad as CMS missionaries.

But the years after the famine saw a steady increase in the number of Irish missionaries going abroad on behalf of CMS: by 1858, the number was four; by 1866, less than twenty years after the famine ended, that number had reached eight; in 1897, CMS sent ten men and nine women overseas.

In today's environment, it is difficult to imagine that missionary work was virtually neglected in all the Reformation churches from the beginning of the sixteenth century until the end of the seventeenth century (and even later in some cases). The Reformation in Ireland dates from 1536, but the first Anglican missionary societies did not appear until the founding of the Society for the Promotion of Christian Knowledge (SPCK) in 1698 and the Society for the Propagation of the Gospel (SPG, now USPG) in 1701. The SPG came to Dublin in 1714 and early SPG missionaries from Ireland included Bishop George Berkeley (1685-1753), who went to Rhode Island in 1728, but returned to Ireland after three years when his proposals for Barbados failed to attract support; and Charles Inglis (1734-1816), who became the first colonial bishop in 1787 as Bishop of Nova Scotia and planned missionary work among the Mohawks.

But in its early years, the SPG confined its work to the colonies and missionary work was often no more than extension of chaplaincy work in the colonies. The Church Missionary Society was founded as a voluntary society in 1799 and its Irish branch, the Hibernian Church Missionary Society (HCMS, now CMS Ireland), only dates from 1814.

Edward Nangle's missionary work in Achill, beginning in 1834, was aimed primarily at Irish-speakers and must be appreciated not only in the context of the wider, general hopes for a 'Second Reformation', but also in the overall context of English-speaking Anglican missionaries reaching out primarily to the non-English-speaking parts of the Empire in the first half of the last century.

Missionary work can be said to have become an active concern of Anglicans and the Anglican churches only as late as the last century. In the past, the growth in missionary activity from the middle of the last century has been attributed in part to the enthusiastic Victorian response to the charisma surrounding David Livingstone and his appeals in Cambridge and Oxford for students to volunteer to go to Africa. More sceptical historians have tried to link the surge in missionary enthusiasm in Ireland after the 1860s to the disestablishment of the Church of Ireland: young ordinands, with fewer career opportunities in the disestablished church, now looked favourably on missionary careers that offered the opportunity of preferment, albeit as bishop of a missionary diocese.

However, both arguments have their weaknesses. Those clergy whose job prospects diminished in the wake of disestablishment were, in many cases, English clergy who had sought sinecures in Ireland, while the Irish missionaries who went abroad often had good job prospects at home: missionaries like Dr Harpur of Egypt, Bishops Russell, Moloney, Hind and Curtis of China, Bishops Heaslett and Walsh in Japan and Bishop Linton of Persia, spring to mind as missionaries who would have had equally successful careers at home.

In addition, Livingstone had little impact on the Church of Ireland and three mission societies that arose after the UMCA appear to have been completely home-inspired: the Leprosy Mission, the Dublin University Fuh-Kien Mission (later the DUFEM) and the Dublin University Mission to Chota Nagpur. As Thomas McDonald has pointed out, TCD in the late 1880s was not 'becoming mission-minded for the first time. Rather, its missionary zeal was becoming more organised ...'

It needs to be argued that many of the missionaries from Ireland who went overseas in the second half of the last century were inspired to offer themselves for missionary work from an altruism inherent in the post-famine generation. Like Dr Adams of Achill, Dr C.E.H. Orpen, founder of the Claremont Institute in Glasnevin, gave up a high-profile career in Dublin at the height of the famine in 1848 to join the SPG missions in southern Africa, where he was ordained shortly after he arrived in the Cape Colony with his whole family. William Homan Turpin, another SPG missionary in South Africa, was confronted shortly after his arrival with a major famine wreaking catastrophe among the Xhosa people following the great cattle slaughter. The work of Turpin and other missionaries may well have been built on the Irish famine experiences; it certainly enhanced the image of the Anglican missionaries among the Xhosa and other people and played a contributing role in shaping the present Anglican church in South Africa. Neither Orpen nor Turpin, nor the other SPG-linked missionaries can be seen in the same light as Nangle or Dallas. But the famine must have had an influence on the social thrust of Irish missionary work in the decades that followed.

The Role of the Clergy in the Great Famine

Robert McCarthy

No event in Irish history has proved so powerfully long-lived in popular mythology as the Great Famine, the 150th anniversary of whose onset we are commemorating this year. Probably no aspect of that famine has been so misrepresented by that mythology than the role of the clergy of the Church of Ireland. A good example of what we have to contend with is provided by a comment by Monsignor D'Alton in his *History of the Archdiocese of Tuam* (1928). 'Nor was the landlord or parson, except in rare cases, moved to compassion or to relief in these seasons of frequently recurring distress.' Nothing could be further from the truth – and happily this is now accepted by all recent historical commentators, including Roman Catholic historians.

As Mary Daly has pointed out in *The Famine in Ireland* (1986), 'evidence of Church of Ireland involvement is best indicated by the fact that in the year 1847 (alone) forty Protestant clergy died from famine fever.'

Of all the groups engaged in charitable works during the famine years, none emerges with greater credit than the Society of Friends, both in Dublin and in London. To them belongs the credit of establishing a network of soup kitchens throughout the distressed areas which kept many thousands alive before the government got round to setting up its own network. Not only did the Quakers set up their own feeding stations, they also channelled large sums of money, raised mostly in England, to the Relief Committees which sprang up all over Ireland. And it is not accidental that the Relief Committees, aided by the Friends, were almost all headed by clergy of the Established Church. The Friends were quite open about their reasons for doing so – given that most landlords in the distressed areas were absentees, the involvement of 'a middle-class trustworthy person, intelligent and possessing good business habits' was essential. The role of the curate of Ballinakill, Co Galway, who acted as Secretary of the Renvyle Relief Committee, was described thus by William Forster, one of the Quakers supervisors, and may be taken as a paradigm of what his hard-pressed clerical brethren were accomplishing all along the western sea-board:

> 'A gentleman of whose exertions and devoted sacrifices and of those of his lady, I can hardly speak sufficiently highly. His cottage, in which he had set up a soup kitchen, was mobbed like a poorhouse on relieving days – hungry faces staring in at the windows, obliging the family to eat their own dinner by stealth.'

When the nearby Rector of Westport, the Revd Patrick Pounden, died of fever contracted in relief work, it was revealed that he had been giving £7 a week (more than half his stipend) to the local Relief Committee, choosing to 'mortgage his life for his fellow creatures.'

To move the focus away from the west, we find that the Revd John Marchbanks, curate of Stratford-on-Slaney, Co Wicklow, died in 1847 only a year after his ordination because 'he starved himself, giving his food away and when the fever seized him he had no strength to fight against it and died almost at once' (C.L. Chavasse). In Donegal, the Revd William Archer Butler, Rector of Raymochy, was also secretary of his local Relief Committee and died of famine fever at his Rectory in 1848, aged thirty-four.

The fact was that social leadership of this kind had long been the preserve of the clergy of the Established Church, something that was increasingly resented by the Roman Catholic clergy. Thus in the local famines of 1817, 1822 and 1831, Archbishop Power Le Poer Trench of Tuam laboured diligently to help the poor of Connacht – for example he paid for a soup kitchen in Tuam itself, served there daily himself, and received the public thanks of the Roman Catholic Archbishop for so doing.

When in the much more severe famine of 1845-48 the clergy found themselves once again having to organise relief, they inevitably faced charges of unworthy motives when forced by scarcity of supplies to distinguish between the most deserving and the less deserving. In the spring of Black 47 public hostility was often the lot of the parsons and their families who manned the soup kitchens. Our clergy bore this opprobrium nobly – 'they knew the workings of the peasant mind and grimly reckoned with the uncomfortable lot that was going to be theirs' (D. Bowen).

Hunger and starvation also stalked the poorer areas of the city of Dublin during the famine years and again the clergy of the Church of Ireland took an active part in relief measures. They decided to pool their parochial resources by jointly founding the Dublin Parochial Association at a meeting in the Chapter House of Christ Church in 1847 to relieve the poor of all denominations – the purpose of the Association being stated to be 'to assist the parochial clergy by equalising the distribution of charity throughout the city.'

Of all the distressed areas, perhaps West Cork provided some of the most harrowing scenes and here the work and witness of the clergy was truly sacrificial. In West Cork a significant proportion of the poorest classes belonged to the Church of Ireland. The situation in Schull and Ballydehob was so bad in the spring of 1847 that two clerical cousins, the Revd Frederick Trench, curate of Modreeny in Co Tipperary, and the Revd Richard Chenevix Trench, then a vicar in England but later

Archbishop of Dublin, volunteered to come and, at their own expense, to set up soup kitchens to feed the starving. Eventually they were feeding 5,000 people daily. A local Roman Catholic priest asserted that mortality in the area would have been doubled were it not for the Trench's 'who had·not made the least attempt to interfere with the religious faith of the people'. In April 1847 the Rector of Schull, Dr Traill, was among those who died from famine fever. Further west in the Mizen Peninsula, the exploits of the Rector of Kilmoe, the Revd William Fisher, formed the basis of a moving play, 'The Apostasy of Matthew Sullivan' by Eoghan Harris, which was performed at a recent Galway Arts Festival. Contrary to what the title might suggest, proselytising was not what Mr Fisher was about (at least during the Famine). He had been supplied with considerable funds for relief from charitable sources in England and he determined to benefit only the poorest classes and not the farmers and shop-keepers, who actually prospered during the famine years.

Like most people at the time he was opposed to giving money as a 'Dole' and so he determined to set the people to build an additional church in a remote part of his extensive parish.

He insisted that it should be done entirely by manual labour – no horses or carts were to be employed as this would have benefited the farmers. Most appropriately the resulting church was – and is – called *Teampul na mbocht* – 'the church of the poor'.

This is perhaps the moment to face squarely the charge of 'souperism' which is still levelled against the Church of Ireland in relation to its actions during the famine period – Professor Desmond Bowen has investigated the matter fully in his book, *Souperism: Myth or Reality* (1970). His conclusion is that it did occur in the case of some members of ultra-Protestant proselytising agencies, notably that led by Alexander Dallas of the Irish Church Missions, although even in his case it is difficult to prove. However, the great majority of clergy of the Established Church were successful in resolving any tensions which arose from being both Protestant ministers and resident gentlemen. They tried to keep their identities in balance and when they did so they were seldom accused of either proselytism or souperism. Rather they were respected as men who brought direct temporal and indirect spiritual blessings to the Irish countryside.

Perhaps the most judicious summary of it all is provided by Fr Ambrose Macauley in his 1994 biography of William Crolly, who was Roman Catholic primate from 1834 to 1849:

> Most of the charitable work done by religious groups during the famine transcended denominational lines.
>
> Clergy of the Established Church, in parts of Ireland where their congrega-

tions were small, helped the destitute Catholics in their districts and the Society of Friends won particular esteem for their selfless dedication to relief. However there was another element involved in relief work which has passed into folklore as souperism, namely the distribution of food and alms by Protestant missionaries to those who would embrace their faith.

Though not extensive, this form of proselytism gave serious offence, not only to Catholics but also to many Protestants.

Church of Ireland mortality during the famine

Cormac Ó Gráda

Though the death toll from the Great Irish Famine will never be known with precision, historians argue for a figure of one million. That figure makes the Great Famine proportionately one of the worst famines in world history. The victims were overwhelmingly the landless and near-landless poor; farmers, landed proprietors, and urban dwellers were less at risk. However, given the crude state of medical technology in the 1840s, medical practitioners, clergymen of all denominations, and generally those who came into contact with the poor in the course of their work during the crisis were also disproportionately represented among the famine dead. Deaths followed a marked east-west gradient, being greatest in counties along the western seaboard, and fewest in counties along the east coast. Yet recent research suggests that no county in Ireland escaped entirely.

What was the impact of the Great Famine on members of the Established Church (as it then was)? How many of them were numbered among the famine dead? Again we will never know precisely, though since Protestants were on the whole better off and tended to live in less affected areas, the presumption must be 'not many'. Nevertheless, as I shall show in this short article, Protestants were not immune.

The use of parish registers as a source for the social and economic historian (and not merely the genealogist) has long been recognised outside Ireland. In France, parish registers have provided the basis for pathbreaking studies on social mobility, population trends, and cultural shifts. That Irish historians have been slower to invoke registers than their English and French colleagues may be largely explained by the poorer quality of Irish registers. Still, over the last decade or two, several interesting studies based on Irish registers have been published. They concern topics such as birth rates and marital fertility before the famine, the incidence of illegitimacy and prenuptial conceptions, and the seasonality of births and marriages.

Here I describe the impact of the Famine as seen in a small selection of Church of Ireland parish registers. Many of these registers survive. Some that refer to the famine period are still in parish custody, but most have been deposited in the Representative Church Body library in Churchtown, Dublin 14.

In the nineteenth century, the registers of the Church of Ireland tended to be better kept and to provide more detail than Catholic registers. One big advantage for the historian is that, unlike Catholic registers, they include information on burials.

Moreover, the ages of the deceased are nearly always given. A sense of the pattern of mortality by age and gender may therefore be inferred from them. The trend in births is also useful information. In this case, Catholc registers provide the necessary detail, and analysis by S.H. Cousens, Joel Mokyr, and others has highlighted the huge impact of the crisis on the birth rate. In this short article I will describe the effect of the famine on two areas, as reflected in their Church of Ireland parish registers.

Let us consider the effect of the crisis on Dublin. Today Dublin contains one-fifth of the island of Ireland's population, but on the eve of the Great Famine its quarter of a million inhabitants accounted for less than three per cent of the island's total. Moreover, the impact of the famine on Dublin was minimal compared to its ravages in places like Clare and Mayo. Nevertheless, Dublin did not escape scot-free.

Just before the famine, about one-quarter of Dublin's inhabitants were members of the Established Church. Protestants dominated the city's professional and business community, but the city also contained many thousands of working-class Protestants. Evidence that the capital's Protestant poor were not immune from the effects of the famine is to be found in the Dublin workhouse records. The admission registers of the North Dublin Union (which may be inspected in the National Archives in Bishop Street, Dublin) suggest that while the great majority of famine victims were Catholics, Protestants were also affected. On a preliminary analysis, I estimate that about one in ten of Dublin-born people admitted to the North Dublin Union in the early months of 1847, and dying there, were Protestants.

Parish registers allow extra insight into how Dubliners fared during the famine. So far I have analysed the records in the registers of five Dublin parishes – St Peter's, St Catherine's, St Luke's, St Mark's and St Mary's. St Catherine's and St Luke's were southside parishes with substantial working-class Protestant populations. The socio-economic composition of St Peter's, a large southside parish, was more mixed, but its registers show patterns similar to St Catherine's and St Luke's. Before the famine female burials outnumbered male in all three, a reflection of the female preponder-ance in these parishes' populations (58 per cent in St Peter's, 53 per cent in St Catherine's, 57 per cent in St Luke's).

Comparing mortality before and during the famine period, the most striking feature is that mortality rose in all three parishes at the height of the crisis. St Catherine's seems to have been least affected, but in St Peter's and St Luke's the annual mortality rate almost doubled between 1844-45 and 1846-47. Another feature in common is that the crisis seems to have hit males worse than females – a common demographic feature of subsistence crises in history. Proportionately, the very young seem not to have been so badly hit. A decline in the number of births might partly account for this, though at least in the case of the St Luke's registers there is a strong suspicion of a significant proportion of infant deaths going unrecorded. The mortality data in St Luke's during the famine years also include many inmates of Cork Street Fever Hospital; whether many or most of those unfortunates had lived in the parish beforehand remains unclear. Otherwise, across these three parishes the incidence by age differed.

In the largely working-class parish of St Mark's (which incorporated the south docks area) and the more affluent St Mary's north of the Liffey, the effects of the crisis were less evident. We may trace a hint of enlightened self-interest in the decision taken at St Mary's parish vestry meeting of 6 April 1847 to appoint 'a fit and proper person to inspect the poor deceased in this parish so as they may be provided with coffins and interment also to inspect all nuisances and report the same to the officer of health who shall define his duties.'

Church of Ireland parish registers in other parts of Ireland would also repay some study. The trends in deaths in the parish registers for the two neighbouring parishes of Ballymodan and Kilbrogan in County Cork show how. These were then largely urban parishes, and almost two-thirds of their people lived in the economically depressed town of Bandon. The parishes contained a significant Protestant community at the time. According to the religious census of 1834, Ballymodan contained 2,264 declared members of the Established Church and 111 members of other communions (mainly Methodists) out of a total population of 9,532 in 1834. The implied impact of the Great Famine is quite striking in these parishes. The burials evidence confirms that the famine did not kill Catholics only; among Bandon's Protestants the death rate was almost sixty per cent above its immediate pre-famine level during 1846-8.

A parish vestry summoned in Kilbrogan in April 1847 ordered that £105 be raised in parish rates. £50 of this was to be spent on 'coffins for the poor', £50 to be placed at the disposal of the local officers of health, and the remaining £5 given to the vestry clerk. However, in May 1847 a resolution to confirm the applotment was lost 'by a large majority', so it remains unclear whether these sums were ever raised.

I hope these reports from Dublin and Bandon inspire some people to study Church of Ireland registers for further insights into the famine period. Studies of areas where Protestant communities were sparse are less likely to reap easy dividends, though aggregating data from clusters of neighbouring parishes might be worthwhile. Quick perusal of the registers of Dunlavin (Wicklow) and Castlecomer (Kilkenny) also indicate rises in mortality in 1846-8 over 1843-5 in those parishes. The counties of south Ulster offer ample scope for analysis along these lines; so do those of Northern Ireland.

As noted, the registers also allow us to consider the impact of the famine by age and gender. Some studies of modern Third World famines report a relative pro-child bias in intra-familial allocations during crises, and the finding that male mortality rates rise more than female during famines is fairly general. One reason for this latter finding may be the reduction in female fertility – a universal phenomenon – and the associated fall in maternal mortality. Another reason mentioned is that healthy females store more body fat than males, and therefore can withstand deprivation longer.

The evidence on mortality by age is less clearcut. In south Asian famines in the nineteenth and early twentieth centuries, contrary to what might be expected, the biggest increases in mortality occurred in age-groups where normal mortality was light, i.e. among older children and adults. A recent study of excess mortality in Darfur, western Sudan in the mid-1980s, finds that child deaths rose more than either infant or adult deaths.

The Irish registers examined so far suggest that male mortality rose more than female during the famine, but that this effect was not strong. There were no striking, consistent changes in the incidence by age. This is another aspect on which Church of Ireland registers may throw further light.

Famine in today's world

Bet Aalen

'Famine is not an Act of God, nor some set of economic or ecological malfunctions … it is something more like war, it is something that people do to each other.'
— *A. de Waal*

Many people would define famine as mass starvation caused by natural catastrophes and virtually inevitable. Such interpretations are influenced by superficial coverage on the media which often concentrates on the final phase of famine, when crucial systems have collapsed and newsworthy pictures of the starving can be transmitted. We are becoming used, even inured, to scenes of skeletal bodies in our news. The sheer horror of these images engenders pity but not necessarily the involvement, pain and outrage which leads to action: for these to flower we need to understand.

Famine is not an event but a complex process with many interacting social forces at work within it. Starvation is usually the last stage of this process, though definitions of famine by those in the Third World often hardly mention it. Much more central in their descriptions is the breakdown of society. Famine does not necessarily imply a general dearth of food but rather a lack of access (entitlement) to it by certain groups. For example, in the Ethiopian famine of 1973-4 there was little or no decline in the general availability of food in the country. Environmental catastrophes are less significant than is commonly thought. In situations where poverty, lack of human rights and external economic factors have combined to undermine the survival skills and inter-relationships in a community, natural disasters such as drought or crop disease can act as the final straw which leads to large-scale starvation. It is, however, famine-related diseases which cause most deaths and these will initially be in the most vulnerable social groups – the old, infirm and very young and in particular the women who care for them during famine as at other times.

Famine should be differentiated from chronic widescale hunger in the world, sometimes referred to as the 'Hidden Famine'. According to UNICEF statistics, 800 million people face persistent everyday hunger; 35,000 die of starvation each day. Yet the world produces more than enough food for its needs. Even within the continent of Africa there is, or could be, plenty of food for all. The problem is unequal distribution of food. 'The rich world has a glut – of food and obese citizens; in the USA a third of the population is overweight – $33 billion is spent annually in attempts to lose weight.' (*New Internationalist,* May 1995, 'Hunger in a World of Plenty').

Ireland, with the world's highest daily intake of calories, may well have a larger problem.

World hunger and famine are both intimately linked with poverty; it is the poor who generally lack assured access to food and so, ironically, it is often the food producers who die from lack of it. Most communities in the Third World have developed mechanisms for dealing with food shortages caused by climatic difficulties but, from colonial times onwards, their food producers have become involuntary participants in world political and economic interchange, exposed to the impact of world markets without the welfare, education and housing safety-nets which we rely upon in the West. They have little possibility of controlling, neutralising or minimising external factors in the way that they have learned to do with natural phenomena. They have been made vulnerable. To achieve a hunger-free world, these external forces must be identified and actively resisted where they impoverish people or hold them in poverty. An effective response to world hunger requires active and informed world citizens and learning is not going to be a comfortable experience, since it will reveal that we in the West are in fact beneficiaries from world inequality.

Major factors involved in the process of poverty and famine are conflict, debt, unfair trade, environmental degradation and lack of human rights. Poverty and starvation are often seen as self-inflicted, resulting from internal conflicts within Third World nations and therefore beyond our control or responsibility. This ignores the fact that many conflicts grow directly out of colonial practices such as the creation in Africa of entirely artificial states which bypass tribal boundaries, and the promotion of élite or favoured groups/tribes with access to power, wealth and resources denied to others. The perpetuation of rivalries and the arming of factions by Big Power intervention are decisive factors. The turmoil in Somalia is an example of how the 'Cold War' in Europe has impacted on the Horn of Africa. Sierra Leone, created for returning New World slaves and ruled until 1961 by Britain, illustrates the continuing legacy of colonial involvement; rivalries between returnees and the indigenous population have persisted after Independence. Since civil war erupted in 1991, two million people (more than a third of the population) have left their homes and fields; as an *Irish Times* headline (29.7.95) states, 'General famine (is) only weeks away in Sierra Leone.'

Conflict not only disrupts the fabric of society with its delicate survival strategies; it also destroys food production by displacing those who tend the land. Even after cessation of hostilities, it may leave a deadly carpet of landmines which will continue to kill and maim and may de-utilise agricultural land for decades. It is estimated that there are over 100 million unexploded landmines still laid in 60 countries. 'They wreak havoc on whole communities, they kill active family members or make them dependent. They turn fertile land into dangerous wasteland where no food can be grown. They force people to migrate and they prevent the return of refugees after war,' states Hean Vathy, a Cambodian Christian Aid partner.

No attempt to understand the reality of world poverty and the likelihood of an increase in famine situations can avoid grappling with the issue of International Debt. Not only is there a stark imbalance in wealth and resources between the West and the Third World (the Third World has 76% of the world's population but only 24% of its wealth), but there is also a very substantial continuing flow of both towards the West. Third World Debt now stands at $1.9 trillion; poor countries make cash transfers to Western banks and institutions totalling $16.5 billion per month/$542 million per day. This amounts to four times the total aid received by the Third World and four times as much as its governments spend altogether on health, sanitation, water, education and transport services. (*The Facts of Life and Debt*, Debt & Development Coalition, Ireland).

Debts were incurred in the 1970s when Western banks, bursting at the seams with money from the oil boom, were inviting borrowing at very low interest rates. Some will recall the invitations in our own local banks to indulge in a borrowing bonanza. 'Why wait?' read the Visa card adverts, 'You can have it now'. In the 80s, when interest rates shot up, Third World states who had borrowed were caught in a spiral of increasing debt, unable to keep up even with interest repayments. Julius Nyrere of Tanzania, visiting Britain in 1985, stated: 'Africa's debt burden is intolerable. We cannot pay. You know it and all our creditors know it. It is not a rhetorical question when I ask, should we really let our people starve so that we can pay our debts?'

Threatened with a global economic crisis, the International Monetary Fund (IMF) came up with a 'package' – further loans to pay off the interest deficit on condition that the country's economy was 'adjusted' to produce the necessary cash. Structural Adjustment Programmes (SAPS) were introduced. These involve severe cuts in government spending on services, removal of food subsidies, currency devaluation, increased taxes, wage freezes and removal of tariffs to allow in foreign goods. This involves a severe shift away from producing food for home consumption towards cash crops for export. So people produce less for themselves to eat, food is more expensive to buy, while their money has less value and must anyway be used on taxes and essential medicines etc. What they produce at home must compete with cheap and often subsidised foreign goods and so brings in less money. What looks like good economic recovery strategy (that is if you accept that a *laissez faire*/trickle down system is the only possible one for our world!) is the 'kiss of death' to the poor on whom it is imposed. The rich élites may benefit and GNP may go up, but the poor are being set up for starvation. Vulnerability is being directly created by eroding traditional methods of survival. Maude Mugisha, who works for a network of women's organisations in Uganda, spoke during her recent visit to Ireland, of the fact that high protein beans traditionally cultivated by women to feed their families, particularly during times of shortage, has become a cash crop; it is now farmed by men for export, sold to traders while still growing and subject to price fluctuations as well as the middleman's rakeoff. (Uganda once called 'the Jewel of East Africa' is now one of the four poorest nations in the world).

Appeals for debt to be written off for the most seriously impoverished nations are sidelined as naïve but the moral dilemma here is age old: 'Does the end justify the means?' Is the death of millions from hunger, whether in famine situations or not, acceptable to achieve an economic order which we may well find is flawed and which is, certainly in its present form, based heavily on the materialistic 'ideals' of acquisition, profit-motive and consumerism?

The problem of debt relates very closely to that of trade and here also we find a situation which is heavily loaded to benefit the West at the expense of Third World countries. A glance at the table of profit percentages on any commodity reveals a startling imbalance. Only 15% of the profit on a bar of chocolate sold in the UK is retained in the cocoa-growing country; a mere £350 out of a profit of £2,500 goes to shrimp farmers in Bangladesh, while the shrimp factory workers receive 30p a day. Most profit from any product comes from its processing; a system of tariffs ensures that this is normally done in the West; quotas prevent more than a limited amount of finished goods entering the EU. The profits raked off by Transnational Companies (TNCs) who control so much of world trade is grotesquely large. The top four TNCs together have an annual turnover greater than that of the whole of Africa.

The growing of cash crops and the heavy dependence on one major crop, which make Third World countries so vulnerable to price fluctuations, were not invented by the IMF; they were usually introduced by colonial powers to provide food for the European table. They have, however, been much emphasised by Structural Adjustment policies. Uganda was encouraged to step up coffee production; so were several other countries. The resulting glut of coffee drove world prices down, nice for our weekly shopping bill but disaster for producing countries! Uganda earns 90% of its foreign cash from coffee; between 1978 and 1991 world coffee prices fell by 66%. This pattern has been paralleled all over the Third World. 'Despite increasing the volume of its raw material, agricultural and mineral exports by 25% in the 1980s, Africa's earnings from these exports fell by 30% over that period because of plummeting international prices. Africa's share in the total value of world trade has fallen from 4% to 1% since 1970.' (*Charter for Africa*, Trócaire).

The dumping of subsidised beef in West Africa, which destroyed the livelihood of nomadic herders in the Sahel, is a notorious but by no means unique example of EU involvement in damaging trade practices. Many Third World economies are heavily dependent on the export of sugar cane introduced under colonial rule; the EU has now become the world's leading exporter of sugar (from beet) and its low, subsidised prices can of course 'collar' the world market. How can Third World farmers compete against those in the West with their income and price guarantees? They are at the mercy of the market. In 1985, the US slashed its sugar imports; the fertile island of Negros in the Philippines, totally dependent on the US market, suffered a severe famine.

Two other factors need mention. Famine is unlikely to occur in situations where basic human rights are observed. India is a country where the existence of a free press, which can alert the world to impending food shortage, and of democratically elected politicians, whose re-election depends on their response to such crises, has prevented famine in recent years. (*Human Rights and Freedom from Famine*, Alex de Waal. Dóchas Conference on Hunger and Famine Today, 25.2.95).

Severe climatic changes may act as a catalyst in vulnerable situations but man-made environmental change creates vulnerability. Severe inequalities in access to land, usually left from colonial times, lead to the settlement of marginal lands unsuited to any but nomadic lifestyles (and often lost to nomadic people as a result) or to the cutting down of virgin forest, also under attack by commercial logging and ranching enterprises. Tree removal for firewood and overgrazing lead to soil erosion and loss of fertility. The so called 'Green Revolution', with its high-yield crop, might have been expected to balance the population growth which often results from poverty; but it requires a heavy use of fertilisers and pesticides not generally available to the poor and relies on introduced and specialised seeds that are less resistant to disease and costly at the same time. It has mainly benefited the wealthy and is detrimental to the environment in the long term. Human health is intimately bound up with environmental health; a degraded environment puts the poor at risk and is a recipe for food disaster.

If a central factor in famine is breakdown of the community and its interconnections, including its links with the environment, one of its most tragic consequences is the collapse of family relationships. Descriptions by famine victims of their attempts to avoid meeting relatives because of the obligation to feed them are particularly disturbing. The avoiding of responsibility for any family member, however remotely connected, would be unthinkable in normal Third World society, though common enough in our own.

The most hopeful element of this frightening scenario is the courage, resourcefulness and ingenuity of groups and individuals in the Third World as they tackle their crippling situations. If the will existed, it would surely not be beyond our capabilities in the West to match that creativity with a real assault on world poverty. Deeper understanding of the processes which lead to famine should at least enable us to identify vulnerable groups and situations and pre-empt the outbreak of famine rather than reacting only in its later non-reversible stages.

Looking at the past

Kenneth Milne

In the *Irish Times* on 16 May 1995, the religious affairs correspondent, Andy Pollak, writing about the Church of Ireland, remarked that 'in the Republic – and particularly in the Dublin area – the feeling of well-being among church members is palpable.' He continued: 'It was clear from the statements of its delegates to the Forum for Peace and Reconciliation last week that they [the southern members of the Church of Ireland] feel their experience as a respected minority church is particularly relevant in an expanding peace process.'

Yet it is these self-same 'southern' members of the Church of Ireland who have grown up with an awareness of the Church of Ireland's chequered history, and who, if one were to attend to certain Northern voices, are an endangered species. Could it be that a knowledge of Irish history, and of our own Church's past (warts and all), has had a therapeutic effect? Psychologists might well say so, and that to face facts is a wholesome process. It may even have a spiritual value, akin to that of confession which, after all, has to do with confronting unpalatable facts.

Of course it all depends on what you mean by 'facts'. For the thing to be remembered about history is that it is concerned with the *interpretation* of facts, not the mere recording of them. Great strides have been made in Irish historiography in the course of the last fifty years, and this changing historical environment has brought with it a certain feeling of relief from some of the burdens of the past. And not only where the religious minority is concerned.

When some of us were learning our trade as history students, we read about 'the Whig interpretation of history'. It signified an approach to history that saw all major political developments as tending towards what was best in the present. In Great Britain, from that particular perspective, everything had conspired to bring about the (essentially Protestant) parliamentary democracy that prided itself on being the envy of Europe.

But the 'Whig' interpretation isn't the only one. There are many others, including a nationalist one, and a unionist one, each of which regards the present as determined by an inexorable historical process. Nationalists often see the emergence of a sovereign, unitary, Irish state as the inevitable climax; unionists have their own idea of destiny. Professor Stephen Dawkins's 'blind watchmaker' is either a whig, or a republican, or a unionist or whatever!

It is largely because we now acknowledge the pitfalls in the path of an ideological interpretation of history that revision has been the order of the day. Not that some revisionists have not themselves indulged in ideological coat-trailing! But it can only be for the universal good that freshly discovered facts, and even some that are not so fresh, are being scrutinised and old assumptions questioned.

Especially since the fiftieth anniversary of the 1916 Rising, there has been some re-assessment of the canons of Irish history. This has, inevitably, meant that the canons of Church of Ireland history have also come under scrutiny. While to some extent this has been a painful process for some people – as painful as biblical criticism and liturgical revision can be – yet not all was pain.

For if, on examination, the Church of Ireland's past has not proved to be as blame-less as many people would have wished it to be, at the same time it has come to be recognised as more complex and variegated than was once assumed. The role of the Established Church of Ireland in its relations with the British state is now examined in its contemporary European context. On the one hand, therefore, the Church of Ireland's claim, so prevalent in the 1930s, exclusively to be the church of Patrick, is now regarded as over-simplistic, while at the same time, the counter-claim, that the Church of Ireland was little more than the chaplaincy to the British garrison, has ceased to be tenable. Nor ought we to forget that such claims fed off each other.

I may seem (in the manner of Alistair Cooke) to have moved a long way from my opening quotation from Andy Pollak. Not so, I hope, for to some extent the self-confidence of the members of the Church of Ireland in the Republic, that he referred to, owes something to the fact that, as a community, they have come to terms with their history.

There is an awareness that the past is complicated, and that in this complicated past we have played a significant part: a part that has not been ignoble when judged in context. Furthermore, while on occasion the Church of Ireland's stance has been questionable, even by the standards of times gone by, the present generation seeks rather to be judged by its own contribution to the building up of the new Irish state, and on its own record.

Which is not by any means to suggest that we should seek to forget the past. We are not, indeed, responsible for it, but we are responsible for our own attitudes and behaviour today. And it is crucial that we recognise that the light in which we are regarded by the members of other traditions, Roman Catholic and 'Dissenter', owes much to their perception of our part in their history.

One of the objectives set before history teachers is that they should seek to cultivate in their pupils the capacity for empathy. At least until comparatively recently, the cultivation of empathy among Irish children, north and south, was a distinctly selective process: empathise by all means, but within your own tradition! We have now reached a point when we appreciate that empathy is an integral part of reconciliation. Which brings me back to the *Irish Times* article with which I began.

For Andy Pollak's article continued: 'The danger of complacency is never far away.' Revisionism in history can give rise to old-fashioned triumphalism.

It may be seen as providing justification, rather than correction. For if, in our relief at the discovery that our antecedents were little different in many regards from their European equivalents, we ignore the manner in which so frequently they were callous, condescending and cruel, albeit in the manner of their day, we are missing the point.

This series of *Gazette* articles is part of the Church of Ireland's contribution to the marking of the 150th anniversary of the Great Famine. It is hoped, and expected, that historical research and fresh thinking will help towards new understanding of the causes and effects of that horrendous episode in Irish history.

The Great Famine, understandably, became part of the argument for Irish independence, and those aspects of the famine that most dramatically supported the cause gained much currency, sometimes unfairly so. One hopes for an end to such canards as those referring to Victoria as 'the famine Queen', condescendingly contributing £5 towards the relief fund.

More especially for the Church of Ireland, one looks forward to an end to blanket dismissal of landlords as callous perpetrators of eviction, and of clergy as dispensers of soup at a price. There was more to it than that, as these articles attempt to demonstrate.

What we all must strive for is truth, as far as it can be achieved. We should not be held responsible for the failings of our ancestors. But we are responsible for our own attitudes, not least towards those in whose folk memory the sufferings of the famine are imbedded. And we must hope that they, for their part, will be prepared to look again at what may have too easily been accepted as received wisdom from the past.

The Great Famine

Address by
The Most Reverend Dr Robin Eames
Archbishop of Armagh, Primate of All Ireland,
at the Service of Remembrance for the Great Famine,
St Mary's Cathedral, Tuam, on Sunday 3rd September 1995

We have grown accustomed to graphic and horrifying images of starvation and famine in our world – the global village. Almost every day TV pictures of starving thousands invade our comfortable homes. We are shocked and saddened and, as a people, we share the frustration of being able to do so little to meet such need – just as we share a sort of anger that in our modern world, with all its sophistication, such tragedies go on happening. Hunger has been described as the great common denominator of humanity's failure to control this globe. Too often the gaunt staring eyes of crying children, too weak even to plea, are the constant judgement on our generation.

Today we meet in the presence of Almighty God to remember other staring eyes and gaunt expressions – not in some foreign parched land – but here on our own Irish soil. Separated by the years and by the generations, the wounds of Ireland's Great Famine remain a scar on our history. Here in the west, which felt the full impact of the famine, we have come to reflect on a human tragedy for which there are as many explanations as excuses, as many interpretations as judgements.

Objectivity in the interpretation of history is not always an attribute when we Irish look into the past. Sadly, when we read our history, our interpretation conveys more about us as we are than what we have been. It is always dangerous to allocate labels to the past with the benefit of hindsight. By any standard and from any standpoint, the years 1845 to 1848 must be for ever one of the most disastrous periods of Irish history. The suffering and the death, the starvation and inhuman conditions which engulfed that generation defy description. The stain on our countryside and the hurt inflicted on our people during the Great Famine have haunted our national life and coloured our attitudes in a myriad of ways ever since.

What we would describe today as political and social injustices prevailed in the Ireland of the eighteenth and nineteenth centuries. Intolerance and economic repression were daily experiences. By 1841 the population of Ireland was reaching its zenith. According to the census, the population was over eight million and by 1845 it was close to nine million. The potato had become the staple diet of the Irish in a land which was exporting most of its grain and cattle. When the blight appeared in 1845, no great urgency was attached to relief – it had happened before. An Ireland which drew its whole economic strength from the soil contained many people who never even touched coinage, but worked for land, for seeds and for barter. After two seasons of blighted crops, desperate hunger and the resulting diseases of cholera and typhus began to take their toll. In those famine years, Ireland lost over one and a half million people through disease and emigration. In religious terms, most of those were members of the Roman Catholic tradition. The Church of Ireland then, as the Established Church of the land, was not unnaturally perceived to represent an element in society which had much to answer for. Humanitarian relief is sometimes a two-edged sword – there are strings attached. Soup kitchens established here in the west unfortunately on occasion carried with them a denominational imperative: soup came with the price of membership of the Established Church. But the famine was no respecter of persons. In 1847 alone, forty Protestant clergy and members of their families perished. During those dark years, the Rector of Westport, who died of fever, had been contributing more than half his salary to the relief of local suffering. The sense of grievance, nevertheless, was widespread and I, for one, do not seek to excuse so much which was done either as deliberate policy or through sheer neglect.

Today Ireland must be the land in which the healing of traditional wounds and the building of new understanding abounds. We all have a great deal which we must bury in the past – and leave behind us in that past. Today as we remember the Great Famine, we remember not just the untold suffering – we remember the anger and resentment. But in the act of remembrance, can we show the vision, the courage and the Christian understanding which alone can heal the bitterness of our troubled past? Reconciliation is the word of the moment. But reconciliation cannot be only for the more recent past of our troubles, vital though that may be. Reconciliation must embrace the sins of commission and omission throughout Ireland's history.

Generosity to those in need has always been a wonderful characteristic of Irish life. We stand high among the nations when we respond to the needs of a hungry world of injustice and suffering. The centre of our remembrance of the years of famine provides us with every incentive to remember those other famines of today.

In the presence of a God of mercy, we remember the tragedy of the Great Famine. We seek the forgiveness of God for the failure to meet that disaster in ways which would have reduced the unbelievable suffering – we seek the forgiveness of each other for the past as we seek God's grace to build an Ireland which can at last be at peace with itself. Nothing less is worthy of the remembrance of those who suffered and died in the Great Famine. We here reach out to that new world of suffering, for as much as we have done it unto the least of His children, we do it unto Him.

Appendix

Ecumenical Service of Remembrance for

The Great Famine (1845-48)

St Mary's Cathedral, Tuam, Co Galway

Sunday 3rd September 1995

in the presence of:

The Taoiseach, Mr John Bruton, TD

The Most Reverend Dr Robin Eames, Archbishop of Armagh

The Most Reverend Dr Donald Caird, Archbishop of Dublin

The Most Reverend Dr Seán Brady,
Coadjutor Archbishop of Armagh

Very Reverend Professor John Thompson,
former Moderator of the Presbyterian Church of Ireland

Mr. Alan C. Pim,
Assistant Clerk of the Yearly Meeting Religious Society of Friends

Members of the Diplomatic Corps & the Oireachtas

Church & Community leaders

The People of Ireland

Service led by the Dean of Tuam
The Very Revd A. M. A. Previté

Organist: **Dr Desmond Armstrong**

Commentator: **Dr Kenneth Milne**

Flautist: **The Revd Gary Hastings**

Singer: **Mairéad Ní Dhomhnaill**

THE PREPARATION

Introduction: The Dean

The Peace

HYMN *(Stand)*

Through all the changing scenes of life
In trouble and in joy,
The praises of my God shall still
My heart and tongue employ.

O magnify the Lord with me,
With me exalt his name;
When in distress to him I called,
He to my rescue came.

The hosts of God encamp around
The dwellings of the just;
Deliverance he affords to all
Who on his succour trust.

O make but trial of his love,
Experience will decide
How blest they are, and only they,
Who in his truth confide.

Fear him, ye saints, and you will then
Have nothing else to fear;
Make you his service your delight,
Your wants shall be his care.

To Father, Son and Holy Ghost,
The God whom we adore,
Be glory, as it was, is now,
And shall be evermore, Amen.

Opening Responses (*stand*):

DEAN: The God of heaven has made his home on earth.

ALL: **Christ dwells among us and is one with us.**

DEAN: Highest in all creation, he lives among the least.

ALL: **He journeys with the rejected and welcomes the weary.**

DEAN: Come now all who thirst.

ALL: **And drink the water of life.**

DEAN: Come now all who hunger.

ALL: **And be filled with good things.**

DEAN: Come now all who seek.

ALL: **And be warmed by the fire of his love.**

A reading from *The Great Hunger* **by Patrick Kavanagh**
Ms. Rosaleen Carey, Tuam (*sit*)

Opening Prayer: The Dean (*kneel*)

Almighty God, Lord of all creation, you have provided the resources of the world to maintain the life of your people, and have so ordered our life that we are dependent upon one another. As we remember today those who suffered so cruelly from the climatic disasters of the Great Famine, grant that in learning from what is past all may have the will to serve one another in times of need and hunger through the sharing of what we have received in a spirit of fellowship, generosity and love. We ask this for the sake of your Son, Jesus Christ. Amen.

MINISTRY OF THE WORD

HYMN (*stand*)

When I needed a neighbour, were you there, were you there?
When I needed a neighbour, were you there?
And the creed and the colour and the name won't matter, were you there?

I was hungry and thirsty, were you there, were you there?
I was hungry and thirsty, were you there?
And the creed and the colour and the name won't matter, were you there?

A reading from the Book of Isaiah (58:9-12) (*sit*)
The Taoiseach, Mr John Bruton, TD

If you remove the yoke from among you, the pointing of the finger, the speaking of evil; if you offer your food to the hungry and satisfy the needs of the afflicted, then your light shall rise in the darkness and your gloom be like the noonday. The Lord will guide you continually, and satisfy your needs in parched places, and make your bones strong; and you shall be like a watered garden, like a spring of water, whose waters never fail. Your ancient ruins will be rebuilt; you shall raise up the foundations of many generations; you shall be called Repairer of broken walls, Restorer of streets to live in.

This is the Word of the Lord

ALL: **Thanks be to God.**

HYMN (*stand*)

I was cold, I was naked, were you there, were you there?
I was cold, I was naked, were you there?
And the creed and the colour and the name won't matter, were you there?

When I needed a shelter, were you there, were you there?
When I needed a shelter, were you there'?
And the creed and the colour and the name won't matter, were you there?

When I needed a healer, were you there, were you there?
When I needed a healer, were you there?
And the creed and the colour and the name won't matter, were you there?

A reading from the Gospel of St Matthew (25:31-46)
The Most Revd Dr Seán Brady, Coadjutor Archbishop of Armagh

'When the Son of Man comes in his glory and all the angels with him, he will sit on his throne in heavenly glory. All the nations will be gathered before him, and he will separate the people one from another as a shepherd separates the sheep from the goats. He will put the sheep on his right and the goats on his left. Then the King will say to those on his right, "Come, you that are blessed by my Father; take your inheritance, the kingdom prepared for you since the creation of the world. For I was hungry and you fed me, I was thirsty and you gave me something to drink; I was a stranger and you invited me in; I needed clothes and you clothed me; I was sick and you looked after me, I was in prison and you came to visit me."

Then the righteous will answer him, "Lord, when did we see you hungry and feed you, or thirsty and give you something to drink? When did we see you a stranger and invite you in, or needing clothes and clothe you? When did we see you sick or in prison, and go to visit you?"

The King will reply, "I tell you the truth, whatever you did for one of the least of these brothers of mine, you did for me!"

Then he will say to those on his left, "Depart from me, you who are cursed, into the eternal fire prepared for the devil and his angels. For I was hungry and you gave me nothing to eat, I was thirsty and you gave me nothing to drink, I was a stranger and you did not invite me in, I needed clothes and you did not clothe me, I was sick and in prison and you did not look after me."

They also will answer, "Lord, when did we see you hungry or thirsty or a stranger or needing clothes or sick or in prison, and did not help you?"

He will reply, "I tell you the truth, whatever you did not do for one of the least of these, you did not do for me."

Then they will go away to eternal punishment, but the glorious to eternal life.'

This is the Gospel of Christ:

ALL: **Praise to Christ Our Lord.**

HYMN

Wherever you travel, I'll be there, I'll be there,
Wherever you travel, I'll be there,
And the creed and the colour and the name won't matter, I'll be there.

THE ADDRESS

The Most Revd Dr Robin Eames, Archbishop of Armagh

Solo (Traditional)
Mairéad Ní Dhomhnaill

THE RESPONSE

AFFIRMATION OF FAITH (*stand*)

DEAN: Do you believe and trust in God the Father, creator of heaven and earth?
ALL: **I believe and trust in him.**
DEAN: Do you believe and trust in his Son Jesus Christ, who redeemed mankind?
ALL: **I believe and trust in him.**
DEAN: Do you believe and trust in the Holy Spirit who gives life to the people of God?
ALL: **I believe and trust in him.**
DEAN: This is the faith of the Church.
ALL: **This is our faith. We believe and trust in one God, Father, Son, and Holy Spirit.**

Dear Lord and Father of mankind
Forgive our foolish ways;
Re-clothe us in our rightful mind,
In purer lives thy service find,
In deeper reverence, praise.
In deeper reverence, praise.

In simple trust like theirs who heard,
beside the Syrian sea,
The gracious calling of the Lord,
Let us, like them, without a word
Rise up and follow thee.
Rise up and follow thee.

Drop thy still dews of quietness,
Till all our strivings cease:
Take from our souls the strain and stress,
And let our ordered lives confess
The beauty of thy peace.
The beauty of thy peace.

Breathe through the heats of our desire,
Thy coolness and thy balm;
Let sense be dumb, let flesh retire;
Speak through the earthquake, wind and fire,
O still small voice of calm.
O still small voice of calm.

PENITENCE (*kneel*)

DEAN: Let us kneel and recall our disobedience to God's commandments and our failure to do his will as we confess our sins to God our Father:

ALL: **Almighty God, Our Heavenly Father, we have sinned in thought and word and deed, through negligence, through weakness, through our own deliberate fault. We are truly sorry and repent of all our sins. For the sake of your son Jesus Christ who died for us, forgive us all that is past, and grant that we may serve you in newness of life to the glory of your name. Amen.**

ABSOLUTION (*remain kneeling*)

BISHOP OF TUAM: Almighty God, who forgives all who truly repent, have mercy on you, pardon and deliver you from all your sins, confirm and strengthen you in all goodness, and keep you in eternal life; through Jesus Christ our Lord. Amen.

(stand)

DEAN: Remember to share what you have with others, for with such sacrifices is God well pleased.

HYMN (*stand*)

Make me a channel of your peace:
where there is hatred let me bring your love,
where there is injury, your pardon, Lord,
and where there's doubt, true faith in you.
O Master, grant that I may never seek
so much to be consoled as to console;
to be understood as to understand,
to be loved, as to love with all my soul!

Make me a channel of your peace:
where there's despair in life let me bring hope,
where there is darkness only light,
and where there's sadness, ever joy.
O Master, grant that I may never seek
so much to be consoled as to console,
to be understood as to understand,
to be loved, as to love with all my soul!

Make me a channel of your peace:
it is in pardoning that we are pardoned,
in giving of ourselves that we receive,
and in dying that we're born to eternal life.
O Master, grant that I may never seek
so much to be consoled as to console,
to be understood as to understand,
to be loved, as to love with all my soul!

DEAN: Accept, Lord, these our gifts and use them for your purposes of love; through Jesus Christ our Lord. Amen.

Let us now kneel and offer our prayers to God our Father:

Mr Frank Curley, Tuam:

O merciful and loving Father, as we remember the past sufferings of our people in the Great Famine, we give you thanks that in spite of this our nation has survived and been rebuilt. Look in your mercy, we pray, on the millions who are still hungry in the world today and are at the mercy of disease. Grant that in understanding and using our own experience we may have true sympathy with them and do all in our power to bring practical help and relief.

Lord hear us.

ALL: **Lord graciously hear us.**

Mr Alan Pim, Religious Society of Friends:

O God our heavenly Father, you know our needs and you care for us all. We pray for all who deny themselves to bring support and relief to their fellow-beings in times of need. May they always have strength and courage, wisdom and sympathy, and see others through the eyes and love of Christ, who had compassion on the crowd because they were weak and helpless, like sheep without a shepherd.

Lord hear us.

ALL: **Lord graciously hear us.**

Mr James Wani Kaffe, The Sudan:

Almighty God, Father of all creation, as we gather here this morning in remembrance of all who suffered or died through the years of famine in Ireland, we bring before you all who face similar hardships in the developing world today. Grant that the hearts of the those who can help may be always moved to quick and generous help. We ask this for the sake of all your family.

Lord hear us.

ALL: **Lord graciously hear us.**

Mrs Ann Ivins, USA:

Father of all, we give you thanks and praise that you bring good out of suffering and weakness. In remembering today the many thousands who suffered emigration from this island through hunger and want and in search of new hope, we give thanks for the opportunities that were found, the Christian faith that was maintained, the relief that was given and the new beginnings that were made. Grant, Lord, that such signs of your goodness may encourage your kingdom throughout the world.

Lord hear us.

ALL: **Lord graciously hear us.**

Prayer for Ireland, Very Reverend Professor John Thompson

Let your blessing rest, O Lord, upon this land we love. Help us all to constantly pursue your ways of righteousness, justice, liberty and peace. Pour out your blessing very especially on our President, Taoiseach and all who carry the heavy responsibility of governing the Nation. Help, strengthen and encourage all who labour for peace and reconciliation and grant them good success.

Lord hear us.

ALL: **Lord graciously hear us.**

DEAN: Eternal God and Father, you create us by your power and redeem us by your love. Guide and strengthen us by your Spirit that through a better understanding of the tragedies and history of famine times we may overcome the difficulties of the past and give ourselves in love and service to you and one another; through Jesus Christ our Lord. Amen.

The Most Reverend Dr Donald Caird, Archbishop of Dublin:

Let us pray for the coming of God's Kingdom of justice, peace and love in the words he himself has taught us:

> Ár nAthair atá ar neamh.
> go naofar d'ainm,
> go dtaga do ríocht,
> go ndéantar do thoil ar an talamh, mar a dhéantar ar neamh.
> Ár n-arán laethúil tabhair duinn inniu,
> agus maith dúinn ár bhfiacha
> mar a mhaithimidne dár bhfeichiúna féin
> agus ná lig sinn i gcathú ach saor sinn ó olc.
> Óir is leatsa an ríocht agus an chumhacht
> agus an ghlóir tri shaol na saol. Amen.

> Our Father, who art in Heaven,
> hallowed be Thy name.
> Thy Kingdom come.
> Thy will be done on earth, as it is in heaven,
> Give us this day our daily bread,
> and forgive us our trespasses,
> as we forgive those who trespass against us,
> and lead us not into temptation,
> but deliver us from evil.
> For Thine is the kingdom, the power and the glory
> for ever and ever. Amen.

Father, Lord of all creation
ground of being, life and love;
height and depth beyond description
only life in you can prove;
you are mortal life's dependence:
thought, speech, sight are ours by grace;
yours is every hour's existence,
sovereign Lord of time and space.

Jesus Christ, the man for others,
we, your people, make our prayer:
help us love – as sisters, brothers –
all whose burdens we can share.
Where your name binds us together
you, Lord Christ, will surely be;
where no selfishness can sever
there your love the world may see.

Holy Spirit, rushing burning
wind and flame of Pentecost,
fire our hearts afresh with yearning
to regain what we have lost.
May your love unite our action,
nevermore to speak alone:
God, in us abolish faction,
God, through us your love make known.

CLOSING RESPONSES

DEAN:	A blessing on you who are poor.
ALL:	**Yours is the Kingdom of God.**
DEAN:	A blessing on you who mourn.
ALL:	**You shall be comforted.**
DEAN:	A blessing on you who hunger for justice.
ALL:	**You shall be satisfied.**
DEAN:	A blessing on you who make peace.
ALL:	**You shall be called children of God.**
DEAN:	A blessing on you who are persecuted in the cause of right.
ALL:	**Yours is the Kingdom of Heaven. Amen.**

BISHOP: Grant, O Lord, for all who have shared with us in this Ecumenical Act of Remembrance, that as we leave your house, we may not leave your presence: be ever near us and keep us close to you now and for ever. Lord hear us.

ALL: **Lord graciously hear us.**

BISHOP: May God the Holy Trinity make you strong in faith and love, defend and guide you in truth and peace: And the blessing of God Almighty, the Father, the Son and the Holy Spirit, be with you and remain with you this day and for evermore. Amen.

DEAN: Let us go in peace to love and serve the Lord.

ALL: **In the name of Christ. Amen.**

The Contributors

PATRICK COMERFORD, a reader in St Maelruain's Parish, Tallaght, Dublin, is completing a PhD in mission history. He works as a journalist with *The Irish Times* and is Editor of the Foreign Desk.

DR ROBERT MACCARTHY is Rector of Galway Parish and Provost of Tuam and is also a Canon of St Patrick's Cathedral, Dublin. He is the author of the recently published history of the Church of Ireland called *Ancient & Modern*.

PROFESSOR CORMAC Ó GRÁDA lectures in economics and economic history at UCD. His latest books are *Ireland: A New Economic History 1780-1939*, now available in paperback, and (in Irish) *An Drochshaol: Béaloideas agus Amhráin* (The Famine: Folklore and Song).

BET AALEN is Education Adviser to the Bishops' Appeal, and lectures at the College of Education. She also lectures on the New Testament in the B.Th. course for Ordinands at Trinity College.

DR KENNETH MILNE is the official Historiographer of the Church of Ireland. He is a former principal of the Church of Ireland College of Education, at Rathmines, Dublin.